BASIC ILLUSTRATED
Guide to Frogs, Snakes, Bugs, and Slugs

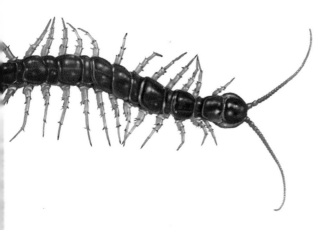

BASIC ILLUSTRATED
Guide to Frogs, Snakes, Bugs, and Slugs

John Himmelman

FALCONGUIDES ®

GUILFORD, CONNECTICUT
HELENA, MONTANA
AN IMPRINT OF GLOBE PEQUOT PRESS

FALCONGUIDES®

FalconGuides is an imprint of Globe Pequot Press.
Falcon, FalconGuides, and Outfit Your Mind are registered trademarks of Morris Book Publishing, LLC.

Illustrations: John Himmelman
Text design: Sheryl Kober
Layout: Maggie Peterson
Project editor: Julie Marsh

Library of Congress Cataloging-in-Publication Data is available on file.

ISBN 978-0-7627-8259-8

Printed in the United States of America

10 9 8 7 6 5 4 3 2 1

For all of you who relocate to the outdoors the crawlies you find in your home, instead of squashing them.

CONTENTS

INTRODUCTION

Some animals are considered universally beautiful. Few of us will wrinkle our noses at the sight of a butterfly fluttering over a sunny meadow. A cottontail rabbit munching on the lettuce in our garden may be forgiven because it is cute. The frogs, snakes, bugs, and slugs of the world, however, don't always get that same respect. The response they often receive is "Eww, gross!"

We know better, though, don't we? We see these slimy, scaly, stinging, smelly creatures for what they really are. Everything about them is designed to help them survive in a world of danger, and they do it very well. We know there is a beauty in that too.

The best way to enjoy the creatures of the world is to get to know them. The more we learn about them, the more we want to learn about them. This book will introduce you to some animals you may have met but may know little about. They all share the great outdoor world in your backyard, schoolyard, parks, ponds—from up in the trees to beneath the soil. Once you come across one, you are likely to come across another. It becomes a treasure hunt you wish would never end. The good news is, it doesn't.

OBSERVING THESE ANIMALS

First, a word of caution: A few of the animals in this book can be deadly. Certain scorpions are an example. While the sting of a bee or wasp may be no more than painful for most people, some are allergic to the venom. Venom allergies can be life threatening. You don't know you are allergic until you are stung, so it is best to avoid finding out! Do not try to handle the stinging animals, and keep a good distance from nests. A pair of binoculars will let you observe their comings and goings without getting too close.

A number of the animals in this book live beneath rocks and logs. Rolling a log is often rewarded with a good find. If you live in an area where there are venomous snakes and scorpions, roll the log toward you, and not away. The same goes for tipping rocks. Lift the rock by grabbing the far end. This allows the creature to escape away from you instead of heading right toward your feet. Always put the logs and rocks back in place. You do not want to destroy the shelter the creatures beneath depend upon.

Night is a great time to search for all kinds of insects and amphibians. Many avoid bird predators by choosing this time to be active. Use a flashlight to search for insects on the leaves, stems, and flowers of low plants. Frogs will often be found along the edges of wet places. Your porch light also attracts a variety of insects, and frogs, which come to feed on them.

A glass jar can be used for temporarily housing your discoveries. A magnifying glass lets you see them even more closely. Many people keep a nature journal with sketches of the creatures they've come across. The act of drawing something forces you to notice details you may have missed otherwise. It also plants the image and information in your brain, the same way taking notes in school helps you remember what you've learned.

A digital camera is another great way to record your findings. If you find something you cannot identify, you can post images to people who may know all about it. There are only 43 creatures in this book, so you will undoubtedly find many things that are not covered here.

Mollusks

Most mollusks live in the water. Clams, oysters, octopuses, and squids are familiar examples. How do slugs and snails fit into this group? Like all mollusks, they have shells. The shell begins as a liquid, secreted by the soft-bodied animal. The liquid then hardens into the many shell shapes and patterns we find along beaches and in our gardens and lawns.

Slugs

A slug may look like a snail without a shell, but many slugs do have shells—they're just located beneath the skin. They eat fruit and vegetables and other parts of plants. If you leave a bowl of dog or cat food outdoors, they'll sniff it out and share your pet's meal.

Two things jump out at you when you come across a slug: (1) They have two long, rubbery eyestalks; (2) they leave behind a trail of slime.

Slugs don't see as well as we do. Their eyes, located at the tip of the stalks, help them sense levels of light. There are two shorter sensors below for picking up smells.

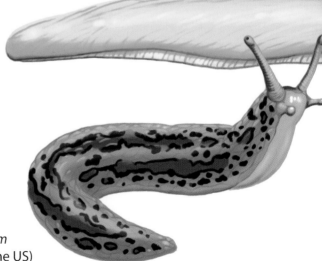

Leopard Slug
Limax maximum
(Throughout the US)

The slime they create has several functions. Mucus keeps their bodies from drying out, and the slime produced beneath their "feet" allows them to climb. The silvery trail also helps one slug find another.

All slugs are hermaphrodites, which means they are both male and female.

Look for their clusters of pale, shiny eggs beneath damp logs.

Dusky Slug
Arion subfuscus
(Throughout the US)

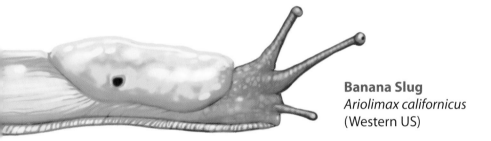

Banana Slug
Ariolimax californicus
(Western US)

Land Snail

Most snails live in lakes and oceans. The land snails had to find a way to keep their body damp while living on dry land. Like the slugs, they secrete mucus. Unlike slugs, they have a shell in which to curl up to keep them nice and moist. Snails are most active at night, when the hot sun cannot dry them out. They eat fruit and vegetables.

We can find snail shells in the grass and damp soil. If we are lucky, we can find one with a snail in it! If you pick it up, it will retreat into its shell until it senses danger has passed.

Like the slugs, snails are hermaphrodites—both male and female. They dig little holes in the soil in which to lay a cluster of eggs. The hole is covered with slime and dirt, making the eggs a little more difficult for us to find.

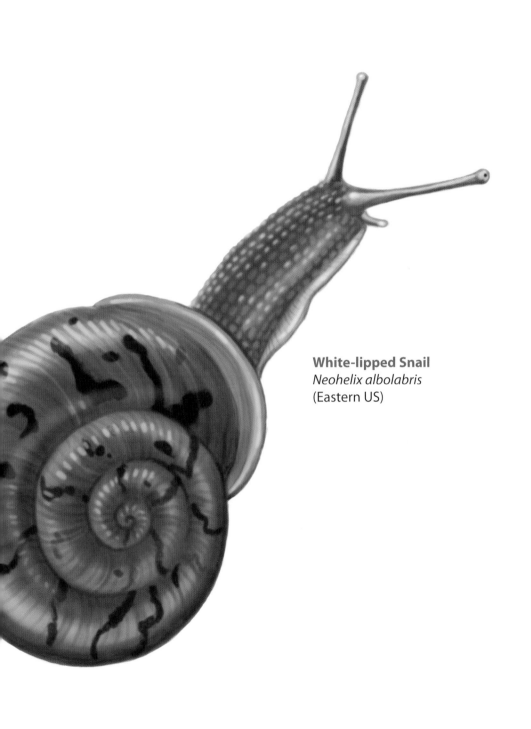

White-lipped Snail
Neohelix albolabris
(Eastern US)

Annelids and Wormlike Animals

Annelid means "ringed one." They are long, legless creatures whose bodies are made up of a series of connected rings. Most of them live in the soil or in bodies of water. Some live inside other animals. Many are hermaphrodites, meaning they are both male and female.

Earthworms

Two of our most common North American earthworms arrived here with the early colonists. While many stowed away in plants the colonists imported, they were also brought here to improve our soil.

The long, ringed earthworm body is covered in a layer of mucus, which helps it absorb oxygen and slide through the damp soil beneath our feet. Worms eat the dirt, from which they extract nutrients.

You can track an earthworm's whereabouts by the circular pile of mud it excretes on the surface. These piles are called castings.

Worms are a common sight after a rainstorm, stranded on streets and sidewalks. No one knows exactly why they leave the ground. We do know that worms can breathe under water for a period of time, so they don't leave because they are drowning. One theory is they use the wet surface to travel faster than they could in the soil. Another suggests that the water increases the carbon dioxide in the soil, so they come up for fresh air.

The young worms develop in cocoons in the soil.

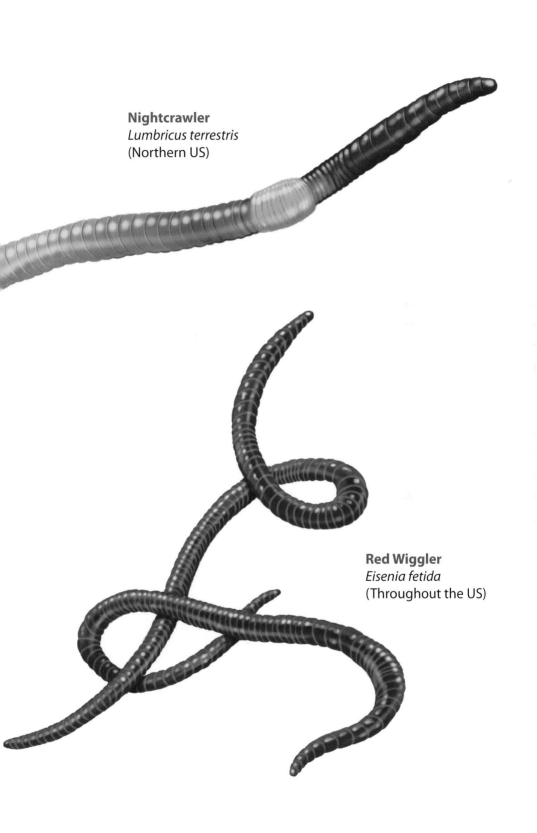

Nightcrawler
Lumbricus terrestris
(Northern US)

Red Wiggler
Eisenia fetida
(Throughout the US)

Leech

Swimming through the water like a ribbon in the breeze, a leech can be seen as a graceful creature. Attached to your leg in a slimy lump as it sucks your blood, it loses that distinction.

These blood-feeders are found in bodies of freshwater throughout the United States. There are many species (some live on land in the tropics!), but a common one goes by the name "American Medicinal Leech." This is the species that was used in past centuries to drain "bad" blood from ailing patients. Fortunately for us, by the time your grandparents were born, doctors had figured out that doesn't work. They are used in medicine today to keep blood flowing in reattached body parts.

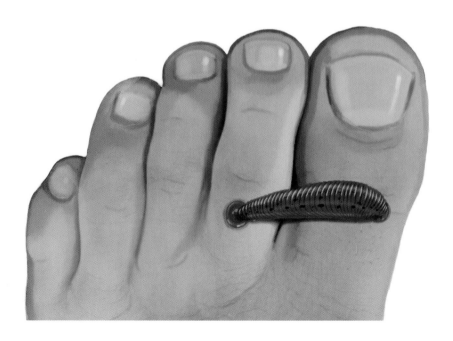

The blood of fish, turtles, and frogs make up much of a leech's meal. It attaches to its host using a suckerlike mouth lined with sharp teeth. The teeth break the skin, which gets the blood flowing. It then releases a chemical, called an anticoagulant (chemical that makes you bleed), to keep that blood flowing.

Young leeches develop in small cocoons on the muddy bottom of lakes or ponds.

Freshwater or Medicinal Leech
Macrobdella decora
(Eastern US)

Planaria

Planaria are not annelids but are instead in the group called Platyhelminthes (plat-ee-hel-min-theez), which means Flatworm.

Planaria have a smooth, flattened body and a triangular head. Most have visible eyespots on top of the head, which are sensitive to levels of light. Unlike most animals, whose inner bodies are hollow, a planarian's body is solid all the way through.

Most live in freshwater lakes and ponds. Some live on land. They eat worms, crustaceans, larvae, and other creatures, living and dead. To feed, a planarian

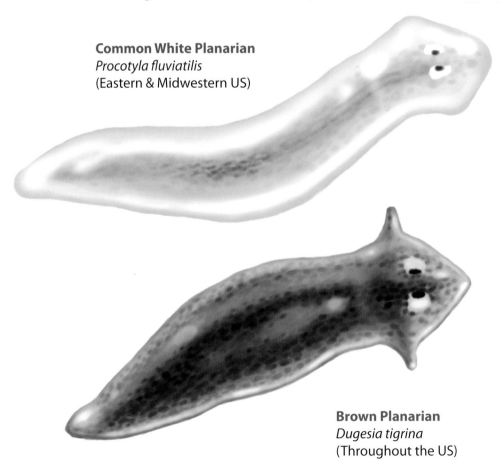

Common White Planarian
Procotyla fluviatilis
(Eastern & Midwestern US)

Brown Planarian
Dugesia tigrina
(Throughout the US)

extends a tube from its mouth, which squirts digestive juices into the animal. It then sucks up the dissolved pieces.

One of the most amazing planaria feats is regeneration. If one gets cut into several pieces, each piece forms a new planarian!

To find your own, tie a piece of raw meat to a string and dip it in a pond. Wait a few minutes and, using a tight-meshed net, scoop out the meat along with the feeding planaria.

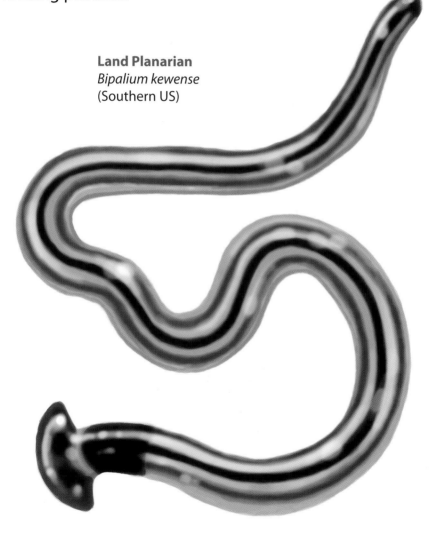

Land Planarian
Bipalium kewense
(Southern US)

Horsehair Worms

Horsehair Worms are not annelids but *Nematomorpha* (nee-ma-toe-mor-fa). They are long and slender, and it was once believed that they transformed into worms

from the hair of horse tails that fell in the water. They are also called Gordian Worms because masses of them form long tangled strings. The name comes from a story in Greek legend about a "Gordian knot" that could never be untied.

The early stage of a horsehair worm takes place inside the digestive organs of grasshoppers, crickets, beetles, snails, slugs, and a variety of plant-nibbling insects. They find their way in when their host eats a plant with a young worm on it. When it is time to leave its host's body, the worm somehow takes control of the insect's brain to make it thirsty. While the host is drinking, the worm bursts from its body and enters the water.

You can find the adult worms squirming and twisting in big tangled knots in birdbaths, your pet's water dish, puddles, pond edges, and toilets (if you've flushed a hosting insect). Fear not! They cannot live inside humans or other mammals.

Horsehair Worms
Nematomorpha species
(Throughout the US)

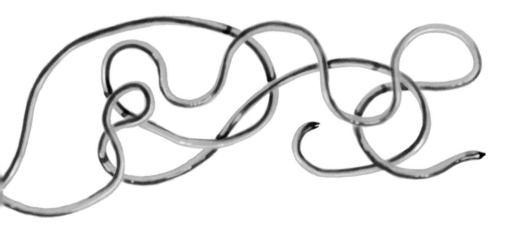

Insects

Insects are arthropods with six legs, a body made up of three sections, and a pair of antennae. Arthropods are segmented creatures with jointed legs and no internal skeleton. Their bodies are protected by a hard outer layer made up of chitin, which is similar to what our fingernails are made of.

The word "insect" means "cut into sections." The three sections that make up an insect are the head, thorax, and abdomen. Nearly all insects have wings. Some wings are used for flying, while some are for making sound.

Most insects start as eggs and go through several phases on their way to adulthood.

YOUNG INSECTS

Spittlebug

Spittlebugs are the nymphs (early stage) of an insect called a froghopper. The nymphs have a tubelike mouth used for sucking up sap from plant stems. As the nymph is drinking, upside down, the sap comes out its other end and becomes frothy as it slides down its body. This nest of bubbly spittle keeps spittlebugs hidden and provides a bad-tasting barrier between them and predators. It also keeps them from drying out.

The adult froghoppers are incredible jumpers. They can jump nearly 2 feet in a single bound!

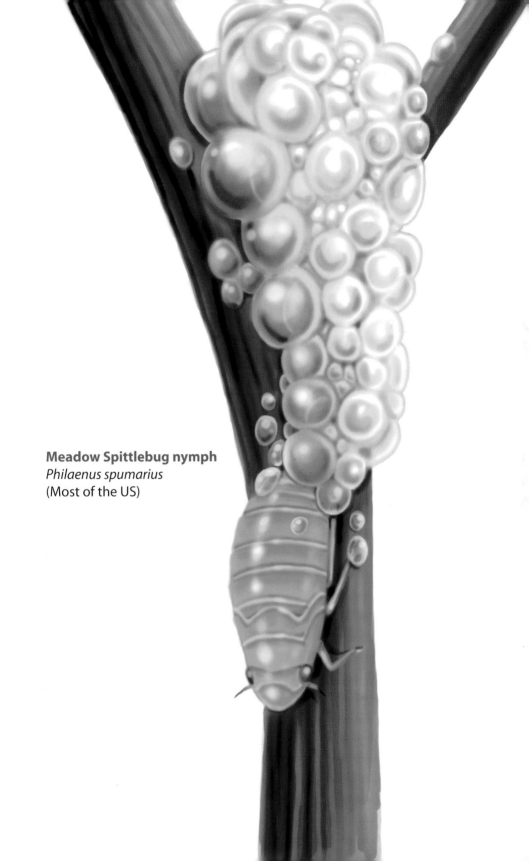

Meadow Spittlebug nymph
Philaenus spumarius
(Most of the US)

Hellgrammite

Beneath our lakes and streams there lives a most fear-some predator, the Hellgrammite. Nearly 3 inches long, it lurks beneath the rocks, at night, waiting for other aquatic insects and invertebrates to swim by. When one gets too close, it is captured in the Hell-grammite's powerful pincers and consumed.

Hellgrammites are the aquatic larvae of dobsonflies. Dobsonflies have some pretty impressive mandibles themselves, especially the male, whose pincers can be up to an inch long.

Fishermen use Hellgrammites for bait, but they must be careful to avoid getting a painful bite!

Hellgrammite
Corydalus cornutus
(Eastern US)

Maggot

If you come across a maggot, there is a good chance that there is a dead animal or rotting meat nearby. A dead mammal on the ground is a maggot's picnic.

Maggots are the larval stage of flies. A larva is the wormlike early stage of certain insects. A butterfly's caterpillar is an example of a larva, but caterpillars eat leaves, not dead meat. Maggots often look like pale, wriggling, pudgy grains of rice. They emerge from eggs laid by the adult flies on their dead, or dying, host.

Maggots are used in medicine to eat away dead skin in a patient's wound. These insects are raised in labs, so they don't spread germs from other, less-fortunate, hosts.

Green Bottle Fly maggots
Lucilla sericata
(Throughout the US)

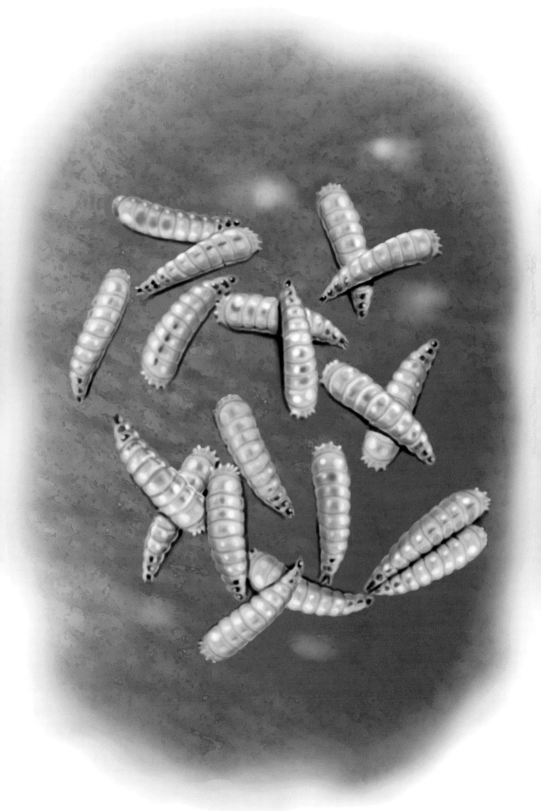

Saddleback Caterpillar

This colorful lime-green and brown insect with a saddle-shaped spot on its back is a moth caterpillar. They are in the group called "Slug Caterpillar Moths." Caterpillars in this family lack legs and move like slugs beneath the leaves they feed on. If you were to touch this lovely creature, you would immediately wish you hadn't. The spines covering those fleshy horns will be driven into your hand, bringing great pain! The venom-filled spines can break off in the skin, causing that pain to continue until the venom runs out. A piece of duct tape can be used to pull out the broken spikes.

Saddleback Caterpillars do not go out of their way to sting you. Their spikes are used to discourage birds and frogs from eating them. When people get stung, it is usually the result of brushing against one while it is minding its own business, munching on a leaf. The sting is not dangerous but may leave a rash for a few days.

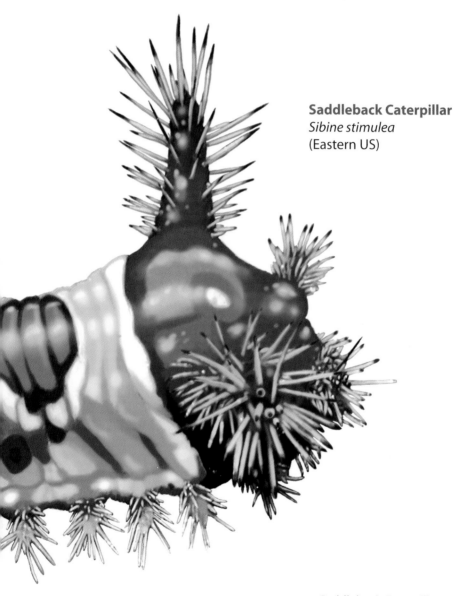

Saddleback Caterpillar
Sibine stimulea
(Eastern US)

Viceroy Caterpillar

Caterpillars have a number of defenses to protect themselves from hungry birds: Stinging spines, camouflage, and poisonous bodies are among them. The caterpillar of the Viceroy butterfly went a different route. It looks likes something a bird already ate!

There are a number of insects known as "bird dropping mimics," but few pull it off as well as the Viceroy.

As if looking distasteful wasn't enough, the larvae feed on willows and poplars, which give them, and the adult butterflies, a bitter taste. They live in marshes, meadows, swamps, and other wet areas with willow and poplar trees.

Viceroy Caterpillar
Limenitis archippus
(Throughout the US)

Pine Sawyer Grub

Grub is a name given to the larva of a beetle. Grubs are found in soil and beneath the bark of trees. One of the larger species, the Pine Sawyer beetle grub, can grow up to 3 inches long.

These legless, segmented blobs are a pale yellowish-white. Creatures that live in places with little or no light tend to lack color, which would be wasted where they can't be seen. Chewing mandibles make up much of their heads. This stage of their life is spent in the darkness

beneath the bark of pine trees, where they carve a network of tunnels as they feed. You can see patterns they, and other bark beetles, make on trees that lost their bark.

You can also hear them as they chew! When digging their winter home in the tree, they make a loud squeaking noise. Years ago, someone said it sounded like a saw, which led to their name "sawyer" (person who saws wood).

Southern Pine Sawyer grub
Monochamus titillator
(Eastern US)

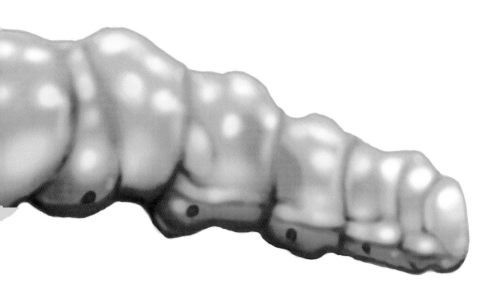

Green Stinkbug

Stinkbugs are considered "true bugs," or Hemiptera. Insects in this group have a piercing, strawlike mouth-part. Some stinkbugs use this to feed on other insects and animals. The Green Stinkbug feeds on the sap from plants.

This harmless, shield-shaped insect carries a secret weapon. When it feels threatened, it pushes a smelly liquid out from beneath its thorax. The unpleasant smell makes a predator think twice before eating it.

The smell has been described as being similar to that of smelly feet or rotten cheese. Next time you find one, give it a sniff and see what you think.

Green Stinkbug
Chinavia hilaris
(Throughout the US)

Cockroach

When people call an exterminator for cockroaches, it's usually for the species known as the "German Cockroach." This is the most common roach in the world, which is not surprising in that a single female can lay up to 240 eggs in her short lifetime.

Cockroaches like dark, damp places. Their small, flat shape lets them slip in and out of tight spots as they feed on our food and garbage under the cover of darkness. They are also known to take the occasional nibble on the fingernails, eyelashes, hands, and feet of sleeping humans.

While they have wings, the German Cockroach is not a good flier. Cockroaches are very fast runners, though, making them very hard to catch when you turn the lights on.

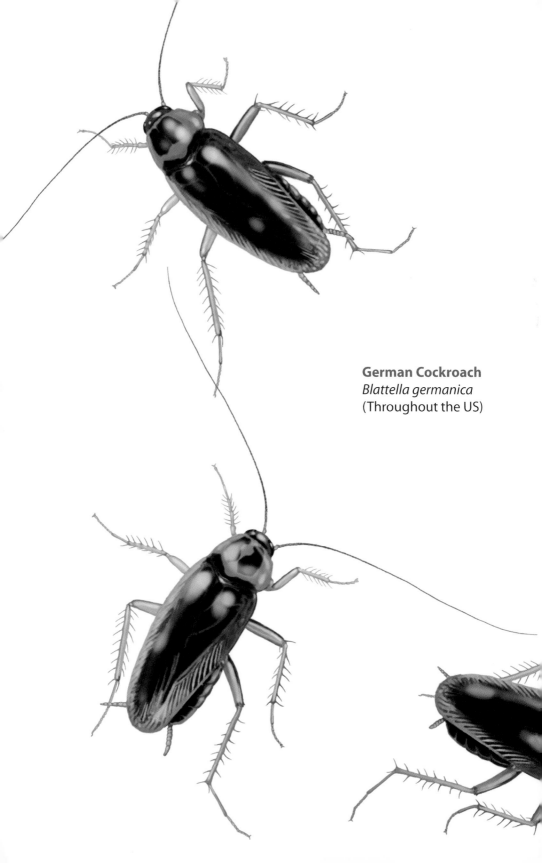

German Cockroach
Blattella germanica
(Throughout the US)

Bald-faced Hornet

Hornets are wasps that live in a colony and build paper nests. The paper is created by chewing up bark and packing it together. Bald-faced Hornets' nests are about the size of an oblong soccer ball. The empty nests are most easily seen when the leaves are off the trees in winter.

You can tell this hornet from others by its white face. "Bald" is an old word for "white."

Hornets eat other insects and fruit. They are very protective of their nests. The female's stinger is filled with powerful venom, making its sting very painful and long lasting! A single hornet can sting many times too. If you see a nest, it is best to observe it from a distance.

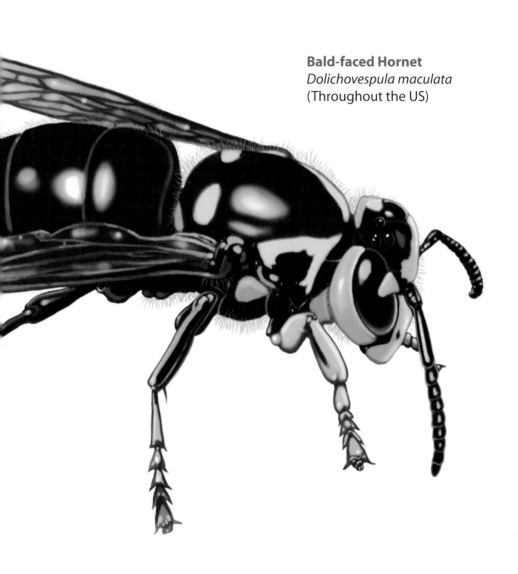

Bald-faced Hornet
Dolichovespula maculata
(Throughout the US)

Yellow Jacket

Yellow Jackets are hornets that frequently build their paper nests underground or in hollow logs. Because of their black-and-yellow pattern, they are often mistaken for bees. Bees, however, are fuzzy. Hornets are not.

If you leave a can of soda or something sweet on the picnic table on a warm summer day, you are likely to have them as visitors. They rarely sting when they are hunting for food. If you do get stung, it's because you accidentally sat on one, or didn't check your soda can before bringing it to your mouth.

Female Yellow Jackets do sting when you get too close to their nest, which is often difficult to see until it's too late. Once one hornet stings, it releases a chemical signal (called pheromones). This calls out to the rest of her family to join her in the attack.

Eastern Yellow Jacket
Vespula maculifrons
(Central & Eastern US)

Paper Wasp

You can tell a Paper Wasp in flight by its threadlike waist, slender body, and long, dangling legs. It is less likely to sting you than some of the other social wasps and hornets. However, as with any in this group, if you get too close to the nest, the females will drive you away!

Their gray-brown paper nests hang from thin stalks. They look like upside-down, inside-out umbrellas. You can see the chambers for their larvae underneath.

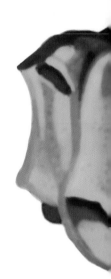

Paper Wasps feed on the nectar of flat-topped flowers and goldenrod. They do catch caterpillars and other small insects, but only to feed to their larvae back at the nest.

You will often see several wasps gathered on the nest. These are the daughters of the female who raised them. They all pitch in to help their mother raise the next generation.

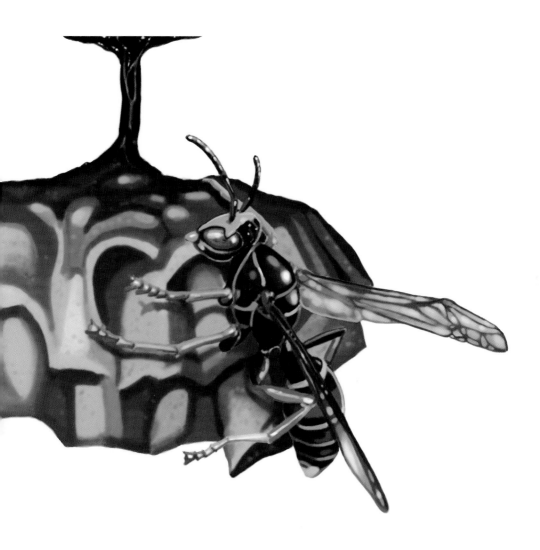

Paper Wasp
Polistes fuscatus
(Throughout the US)

House Cricket

If you want to see House Crickets, go to a pet store. These are the crickets bred to feed pet reptiles and amphibians. They used to be common in people's homes, but as houses became better sealed from the outdoors, fewer were able to sneak in as guests. Many homes, however, are still serenaded with the call of this European cricket. Some cultures believe it's good luck to have a cricket chirping in the home. Some believe it's bad luck. It's only bad luck, though, if they eat your clothes, which they're known to do.

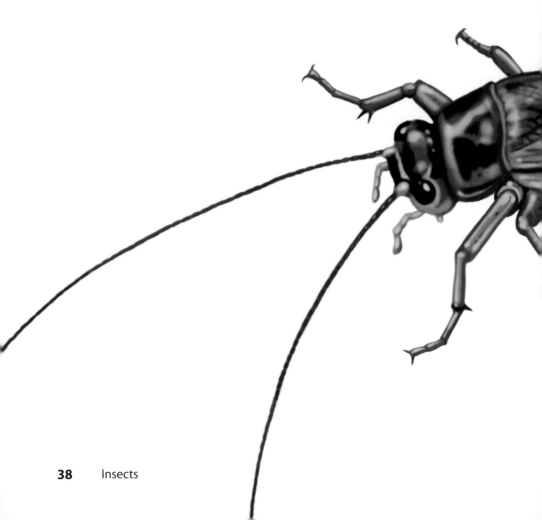

The chirp of a House Cricket is what most people think of when they imagine a cricket chirping—a high, rich, steady "chirp . . . chirp . . . chirp . . ." It is very similar to the song of the field crickets outdoors.

House Cricket
Acheta domesticus
(Central to Eastern US)

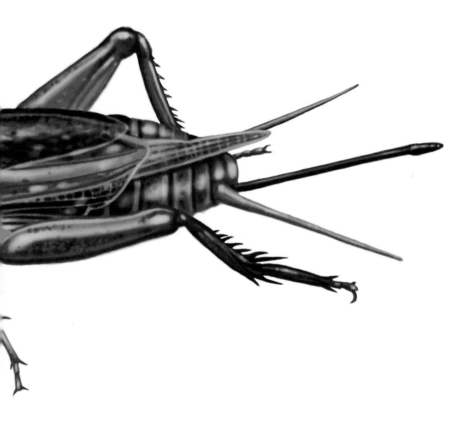

Mormon Cricket

The march of the Mormon Crickets is a sight to behold! When their bodies grow low on salt and protein, they swarm over the land by the millions in search of new sources. Each individual contains some of those nutrients, so the crickets in the front are also marching to keep from being eaten by the crickets behind them.

Mormon Crickets are not crickets but katydids. They eat grasses and shrubs and other insects. Their swarms were first described by the Mormons who settled in Utah, hence their name.

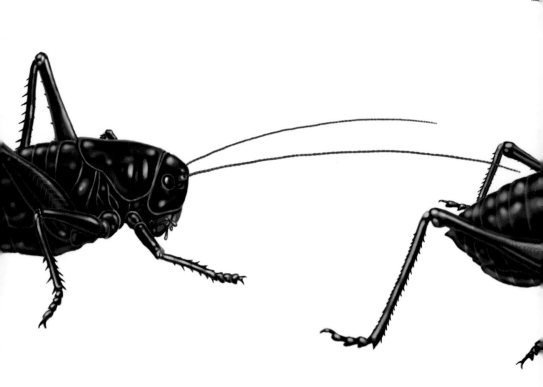

Native Americans used to drive these great swarms into waiting fires and feast on the cooked insects.

Most male katydids will rub their wings together to call females and chase off other males. The call of the Mormon Cricket sounds like a high-pitched rattlesnake.

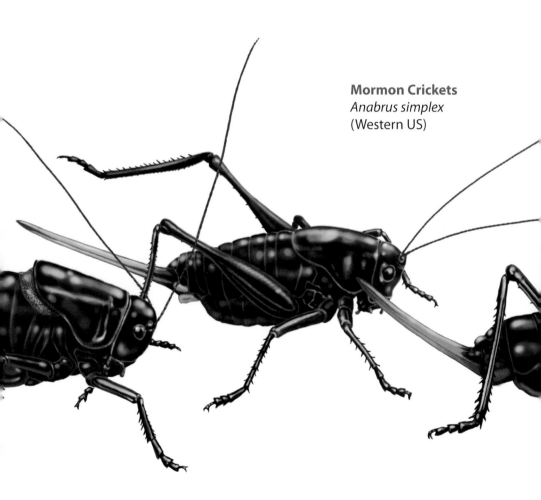

Mormon Crickets
Anabrus simplex
(Western US)

Earwig

It was once believed that earwigs crawled into the ear of sleeping victims and laid eggs in their brain. It was this belief that put the "ear" in their name. "Wig" is a form of an old word, "wicga," which means insect.

While earwigs do like warm, dark, damp places and could crawl in your ear, they don't.

Common Earwig
Forficula auricularia
(Throughout the US)

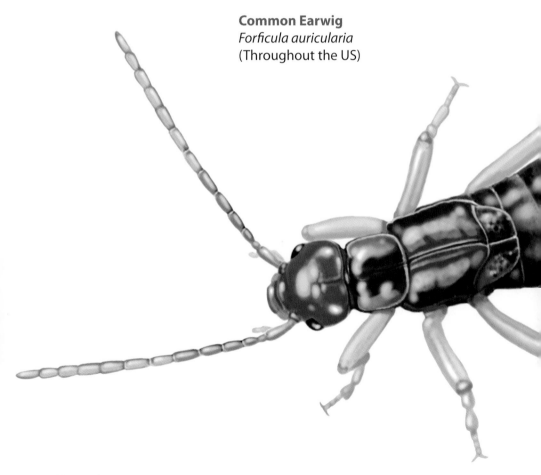

The pincers on the tip of the abdomen appear more dangerous than they are. They are used as a pair of extra fingers for grooming and courtship. They are also used in defense. A pinch from an earwig's pincers may hurt a little, but it won't do any damage.

Earwigs are omnivores, meaning they eat many things, which include living and dead plants and insects.

Mosquito

A mosquito, which is Spanish for "little fly," is often heard before seen. The humming sound is created by the vibration of its beating wings. It lets you know what's coming next!

Mosquitoes do not bite. They pierce. A tubelike mouth breaks the skin and injects an anticoagulant (chemical that makes you bleed). As they drink, their bodies more than double in size.

Only female mosquitoes drink blood, which is used to feed the eggs in their bodies. Those eggs are laid in still water. They hatch into wriggling larvae, which become food for other aquatic creatures.

The females who make it to adulthood find us by sensing the heat in our bodies and the carbon dioxide exhaled in our breath.

Northern House Mosquito
Culex pipiens
(Northeast US)

Dung Beetles/Tumblebugs

Where there is dung (droppings from plant-eating mammals), there are likely to be dung beetles. Tumblebugs are dung beetles that roll dung into a ball. They roll the ball with their hind legs, looking for a spot in which to bury it. Sometimes another tumblebug will try to steal that ball.

The ball is buried in the soil, where the beetle feeds on it. The adults drink the liquid from the dung. Their larvae feed on the dung itself.

Farmers love dung beetles! The beetles bury the manure from their livestock, which keeps the flies from finding it. The manure also fertilizes the soil.

Dung Beetles
Canthon species
(Throughout the US)

Carrion Beetle

Moments after an animal dies in the woods, the flies arrive. The flies lay eggs on that carcass, which grow into maggots. Then the carrion beetles arrive. They eat the maggots, and the carcass, while laying their own eggs. By eating the maggots, they are leaving more carcass for their offspring to feed on.

The beetle larvae hatch and join their parents in eating the maggots and carcass.

American Carrion Beetles are often covered with little hitchhikers. These are mites that drop off the beetle and feast on maggot eggs and small maggots. Then they climb back onto their ride to travel to the next dead animal. This works out well for the beetles. They get some help keeping down the maggot competition. The mites benefit from the free ride.

American Carrion Beetle
Necrophila americana
(Eastern US)

Burying Beetle

The Burying Beetle is the undertaker of the insect world. The beetles have a strong sense of smell and can pick up the odor of a small, decaying animal from over a mile away. The male is often the first to arrive. He claims the carcass as his own. If another Burying Beetle arrives, they fight, and the winner gets to keep it. The male does share it, though, with the first female who arrives. She is often attracted to him by his pheromones (kind of an insect perfume), which he releases into the air.

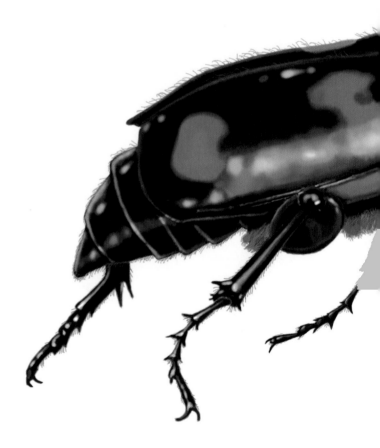

After mating, the female lays eggs in the soil next to the carcass. While the eggs develop, the male and female busy themselves burying the dead animal by digging a hole beneath it.

Burying Beetles are very good parents. They protect and feed their larvae until they can eat on their own. This is very unusual behavior for an insect!

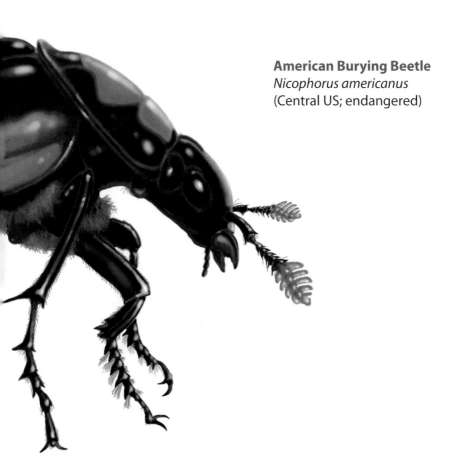

American Burying Beetle
Nicophorus americanus
(Central US; endangered)

Arachnids

Arachnids are invertebrates (meaning they have no internal skeleton) with eight jointed legs. They do not have the wings or antennae found on insects. Their body is divided into two parts—the cephalothorax (seh-fa-lo-thor-ax), which contains the head and thorax (middle section), and the abdomen.

Ticks

When a tick gets hungry, it goes on a "quest." It climbs to the top of a piece of grass, extends its front legs, and waits to latch on to a passerby (this is called "questing"). Once aboard its host, it breaks the skin and begins to drink the host's blood through a barbed beak. The barbs lock the tick in place while it is feeding. Ticks are so strong, that when you pull a tick off your body, you often leave the head behind!

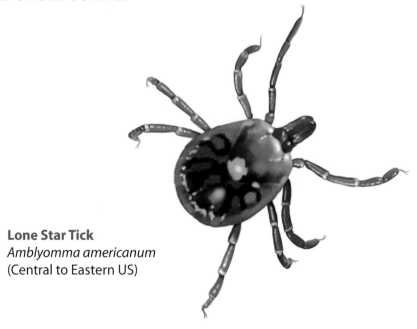

Lone Star Tick
Amblyomma americanum
(Central to Eastern US)

Deer Tick
Ixodes scapularis
(Central to Eastern US)

Ticks go through three stages of development: larva (which has only six legs), nymph, and adult. Each stage only feeds once. When the adult female has her meal of blood, she lays a batch of thousands of eggs and then dies.

Ticks are responsible for spreading more diseases to humans and animals than any other parasite. When walking on a trail, check your clothes often for hitch-hikers. Ticks are best removed from the skin with tweezers. Grab as close to the head as possible, and pull gently but firmly.

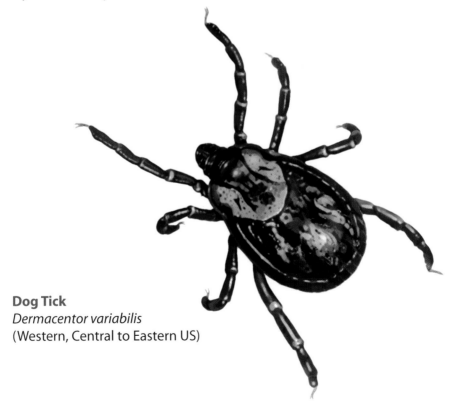

Dog Tick
Dermacentor variabilis
(Western, Central to Eastern US)

Black Widow

The Black Widow is the most venomous spider in North America. The name comes from the belief that the female eats the male after mating. This only happens occasionally.

Black Widows are easily recognized by the red hour-glass shape under the abdomen. The bright red is a warning to birds and other predators that this spider would not make a good meal.

The female builds a somewhat sloppy-looking, but very strong, web. She spends most of her time waiting in the web to snare an insect. When an insect gets trapped, the spider injects her venom into its body. This dissolves the inner organs, which the spider drinks up.

Black Widows do not seek out humans to bite. When bites do occur, it is usually when someone accidently brushes up against the web, or sits on a spider. The bite is extremely painful and can be fatal to small children.

Black Widow
Latrodectus mactans
(Southeastern US)

Argiope Spider

Argiopes (ar-guy-o-pee) are among our largest web-building spiders. Their webs are beautifully designed, as are most created by "orb weaver" spiders. The sticky silk orbs can span several feet across. In the center there is a heavy, white zigzagged line of silk. It is possible that the zigzags help small mammals avoid walking through the webs, which are built close to the ground.

Argiope spiders live in sunny meadows. During the day they wait, upside down, in the web for insects. At night they eat most of their webs and spin brand-new ones. This keeps their insect traps nice and sticky.

Like most spiders, Argiopes are venomous. However, you'd have to grab one to get it to bite you. The venom is not very toxic to humans.

Black and Yellow Garden Spider
Argiope aurantia
(Throughout the US)

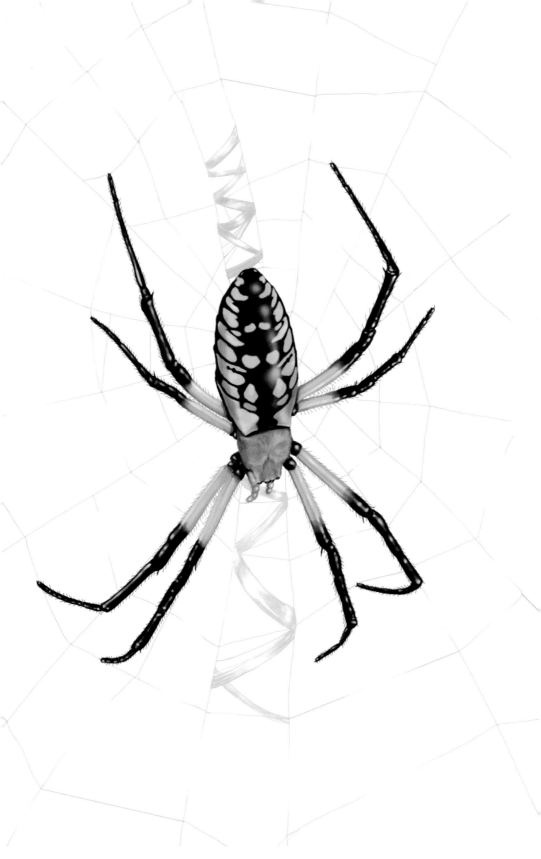

Cellar Spider

If you have cobwebs on your ceilings, there is a good chance your home is host to the harmless cellar spider. The females build their webs in basements, bathrooms, or any room in the house that is kept warm.

Cellar spiders can be tricksters. If one isn't catching enough insects in her web, she will go to the web of another spider and vibrate it with her leg. The spider thinks it's a bug caught in her web and comes out to eat it, but instead gets eaten by the cellar spider!

If you see a cellar spider in its web, poke your finger next to it. The spider will start vibrating and swinging in circles, so fast it becomes difficult to see.

These spiders are venomous, but their fangs are too short to deliver the venom in human skin.

Cellar Spider
Pholcus phalangiodes
(Eastern & Western US)

Daddy Longlegs

Also called harvestmen, daddy longlegs are often confused with spiders. That confusion occurs because they
appear to have eight legs. However, the second, longer,
pair of legs are used more as antennae. Daddy longlegs'

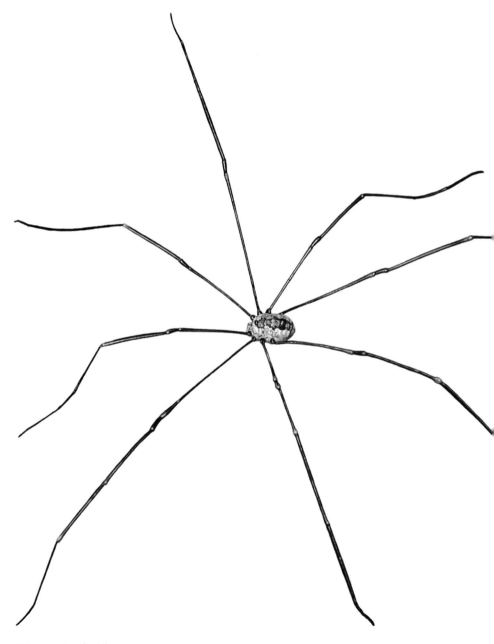

bodies are fused into one oval shape. Spiders' bodies have two sections.

Daddy longlegs eat a wide variety of small insects—dead and alive—and plant material. They do not build webs, but instead wander the leaves in search of a meal. They lack the fangs and venom of spiders and instead chew their food. They are completely harmless to humans.

If a predator grabs it by the leg, that leg easily detaches. The leg keeps twitching, holding the predator's attention while the daddy longlegs runs to safety.

Many daddy longlegs are good dads. When the female lays her eggs, it is the male who stays and guards them.

Daddy Longlegs
Odiellus pictus
(Eastern US)

Scorpion

A quick look at a scorpion suggests that it could give you trouble from both ends. It's the venom-filled tail you should be concerned about, though. The claws, called pedipalps, are for holding its prey as it eats or injects the prey with venom.

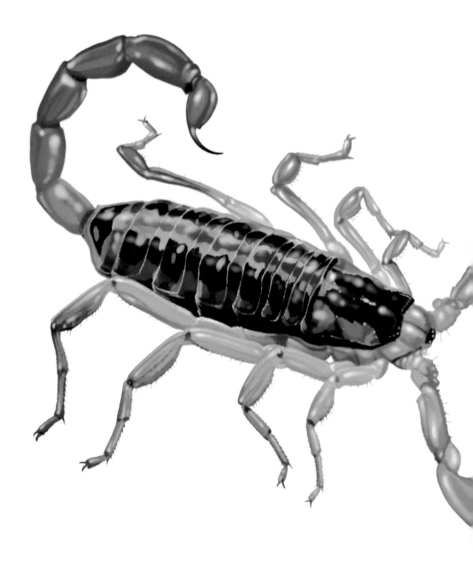

The venom is used to make it easier to eat its prey. It is also a good defense against predators who want to eat the scorpion.

Scorpions spend the day in burrows or hiding beneath rocks and logs. They are most active at night and can be found using an ultraviolet light, which makes them glow!

Young scorpions come out of their mothers alive. There can be up to a hundred of them per brood. Mom carries them on her back until they're big enough to fend for themselves.

While many scorpions have only a mild sting, the sting of some is deadly.

Striped Bark Scorpion
Centruroides vittatus
(Central & Southern US)

Miscellaneous "Bugs"

Centipede

Though the name centipede means "100 legs," most in North America have between 30 and 60. Their first pair of legs are located behind the head, but they don't look at all like legs! They form a pair of venom-injecting pincers called forcipules. These are used to catch and immobilize insects. A centipede's bite can be very painful, like a bee sting, but rarely dangerous.

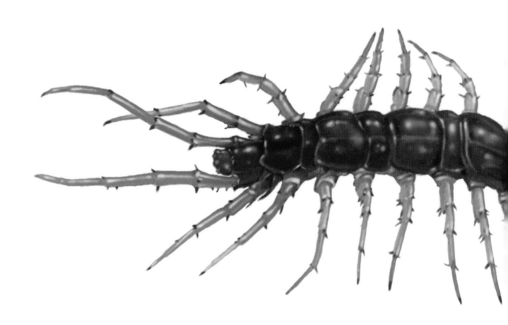

The legs of a centipede stick straight out of the sides of its body. Each pair of legs is a little longer than the one in front of it. This prevents centipedes from tripping over their own feet.

To find centipedes, look under rocks and logs where there is damp soil. They need moisture to survive and will quickly scurry to cover when exposed to sunlight.

Centipedes are among the oldest surviving creatures on the planet. Fossils show that they have been around for over 400 million years.

Stone Centipede
Lithobius forficatus
(Throughout the US)

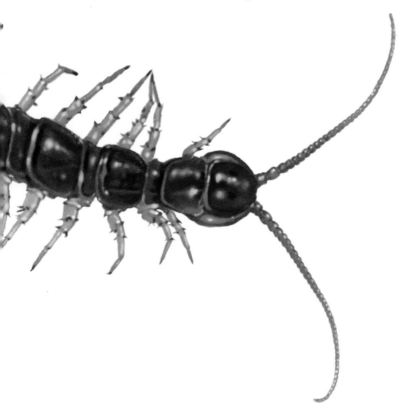

Centipede   **65**

Millipede

Millipedes are often confused with centipedes. Centipedes have one pair of legs per body segment, which stick out the sides. Millipedes have two pairs of legs per body segment, beneath their rounded bodies.

Since they only eat decaying plant matter, they have no need for venomous pincers. Millipedes don't bite, but they do release a foul-smelling poison to discourage predators from eating them.

If they are disturbed, or dying, they roll up in a coil. The segmented outer shell protects the soft body beneath.

Millipede
Family Parajulidae
(Throughout the US)

Like centipedes, millipedes grow more legs each time they molt. They do not end up, as their name suggests, with a thousand legs, but they do have a lot of them—between 47 and 197 pairs.

Pillbug

Pillbugs share the same damp, dark habitat as centipedes and millipedes. However, being crustaceans, they are more closely related to lobsters than those other two arthropods. They even breathe with gills!

These creatures go by many names: woodlice, cheeselogs, slaters, and chuggy pigs. But one name truly describes what makes them so unique—roly poly. When they sense danger they roll into a tight ball. They also do this to keep from drying out. Sowbugs, which look very similar to pillbugs, do not roll into a ball.

Common Pillbug
Armadillidium vulgare
(Throughout the US)

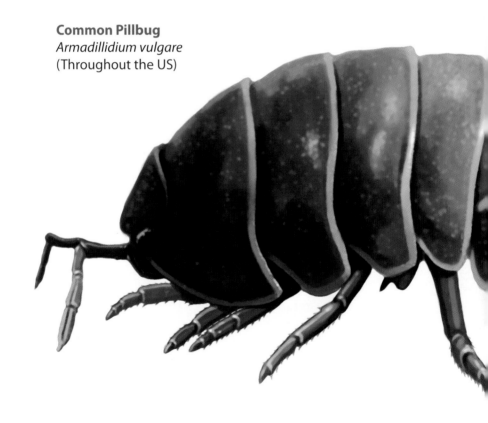

Pillbug mothers carry their young in little pouches beneath the body. This keeps them safe from being eaten while their shells grow harder. They eat dead plant and animal matter and are harmless to humans.

They spend winter rolled up tight and piled together with other Pillbugs.

Amphibians

Most amphibians begin their lives as eggs in the water. They hatch as fully aquatic tadpoles (young frogs) or larvae (young salamanders). Over the next few months, or years, the tadpoles and larvae change form to live on land (some stay in the water). There they feed on insects and other small creatures. Since their skin needs to remain moist, they are rarely far from water.

Frogs are Anurans, which means "without a tail." They have large eyes to help them see in the dark, long hind legs for jumping, and a sticky tongue for catching small prey.

Salamanders are Caudata, meaning "with a tail." They can look like lizards but lack scales or claws (their bodies and toes are soft). Some spend their lives in the water, but others can be found by turning over logs and flat rocks.

American Toad

When you look at the bumpy, scowling face of an American Toad, you may be surprised when you hear its sweet, melodic trill. They sing in and near their breeding ponds in early spring.

Toads are frogs. They have bumps on their skin and two poison glands (paratoid glands) on the sides of their neck; they spend a good part of their life on dry land.

Those poison glands protect them from mammal predators. Unfortunately for the toads, snakes don't seem to mind the poison. You should always wash your hands after handling toads, or any frog.

American Toad eggs are laid in a chain of black, pea-sized balls in lakes, ponds, puddles, and bicycle tire ruts.

American Toad
Bufo americanus
(Eastern to Central US)

Bullfrog

While not really the size of a bull, as suggested by their name, Bullfrogs are the largest frogs in North America. Most of their time is spent in the water, along the edges of lakes and ponds.

Their large size makes them kings and queens of the lake, where they will eat just about anything they can fit in their mouths.

To tell a Bullfrog from the similar-looking Green Frog, look at the ridge of skin around its ear (the ear, or

tympanic membrane, is that large disk behind the eye). If the ridge wraps around the ear, it is a Bullfrog. If the ridge goes down the sides of the body, it is a Green Frog.

The call of a Bullfrog is a deep, "Jug-o-rum . . . jug-o-rum . . . ." If you stand close enough, you can feel the call vibrating in your chest.

American Bullfrog
Rana catesbeiana
(Most of the US)

Wood Frog

Wood Frogs are the masked wanderers of the frog family. Once they leave the water as froglets, they move into the surrounding woods. They remain among the leaves on the ground until late fall, when they take cover in shallow burrows.

In the winter the frogs freeze solid! Very few animals can survive their bodies turning to ice. The organs of Wood Frogs, however, are protected by a sugary anti-freeze produced by the liver.

Come late winter/early spring, the Wood Frogs thaw out and return to their pools to breed. They prefer vernal pools (small ponds that dry out) because they support no fish, which would eat their eggs.

You can hear the males "chuckling" in the water on cool spring nights.

Wood Frog
Rana sylvatica
(Northern US)

Redback Salamander

Redback Salamanders are one of the most numerous and easiest to find of all the salamanders. While there are some that are gray or bright orange, most of them have a brick-red stripe down their back.

They spend their lives under leaves, logs, and rocks on dry land. They are one of the few species that lay their eggs out of the water. Their larval stage takes place inside the egg!

The mother guards her eggs, sometimes wrapping her body around them to keep them damp.

Redbacks are among the group of "lungless" salamanders, breathing instead through their skin.

If you put a flat board in your wooded yard or park, you may encourage these salamanders (and other creatures) to move in.

Redback Salamander
Plethodon cinereus
(Eastern US)

Spotted Salamander

On the first warm, rainy evening in late winter/early spring, the Spotted Salamanders leave their burrows and migrate to nearby vernal pools (small ponds that dry out).

If there is a road between their woodland burrows and their pools, you can go out with a flashlight and find them as they cross. With those bright yellow spots, they are hard to mistake for any other salamander.

The salamanders breed in those pools and then head back to the woods, leaving behind slimy, softball-sized egg masses.

The Spotted Salamanders stay beneath the leaf litter for the rest of the year. Their bodies produce a layer of slime to keep them from drying out. It also makes them taste bad to predators.

Spotted Salamander
Ambystoma maculatum
(Eastern US)

Barred Tiger Salamander

Barred Tiger Salamanders are the largest land salamanders in the world. While they are usually between 6 and 8 inches long, some can grow up to 14 inches! The name "tiger" salamander refers to the heavy striping on the body.

Tiger salamanders are "mole salamanders" (like the Spotted Salamander). They are so named because, like

Barred Tiger Salamander
Ambystoma mavortium
(Central to Western US)

moles, they spend winters in underground burrows. Since they don't have claws to dig, they use burrows made by other animals.

Salamanders are most active at night, when the sun cannot dry out their moist skin. They hunt for slugs, insects, and worms above and below the leaves on the ground.

Reptiles

Reptiles are often grouped with amphibians, but they are very different creatures. Most reptiles have scaly skin. Amphibian skin is smooth. They have claws instead of toes (except for snakes, of course). Their eggs are laid on dry land. Most amphibians lay them in water. When a reptile hatches from an egg, it looks like a miniature version of the adult.

Garter Snake

Garter snakes are among the most common species of snakes. There are many different kinds found all over North America. They are generally medium-sized snakes, not growing much more than 3 feet long. Their stripes help them blend in with their grassy habitat.

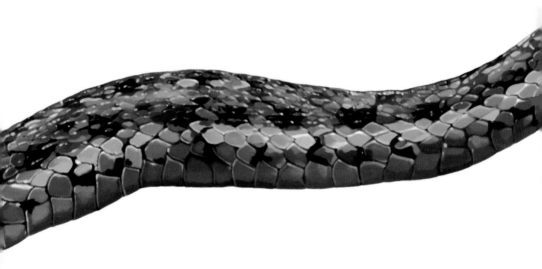

If you handle a garter snake, you will end up with smelly fingers. They release a mixture of feces and a foul-smelling liquid to discourage predators from eating them. They may also bite, but their venom is weak. It is delivered from their back teeth, and they would have to chew for a while to release it.

A garter snake mother does not lay eggs. She carries her eggs in her abdomen and gives birth to live young.

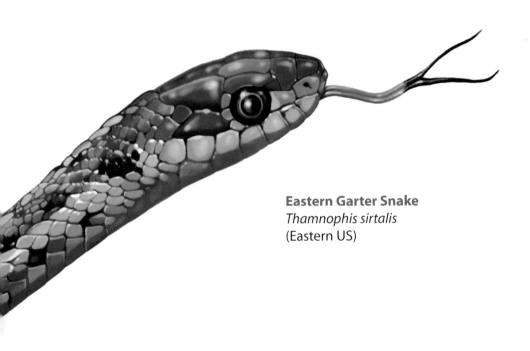

Eastern Garter Snake
Thamnophis sirtalis
(Eastern US)

Worm Snake

If you find a large, scaled "worm" in the soil, it is likely to be a worm snake. These snakes spend most of their lives in burrows, beneath leaves, and in loose, damp soil. They have a sharp (harmless) tip at the end of their tail that is used for digging.

While they are very common, worm snakes' fossorial (underground) life can make them difficult to find.

Like many snakes, they give off a foul odor when handled. They are nonvenomous and have such a small head that if you were to be bitten, you'd hardly feel it. They are very nonaggressive, though, and will wrap around your fingers like a pretzel!

Worm snakes' favorite food is earthworms. The snakes themselves are often food for larger snakes.

Eastern Worm Snake
Carphophis amoenus
(Eastern to Central US)

Anole

Anoles (a-no-lee) are found in the southeastern United States in trees, shrubs, and inside and outside of homes. Many are sold as pets.

These lizards are sometimes called chameleons (they're not, though), because they can change their color. Their color changes reflect their mood, health, and outside temperature.

Male anoles have a flap of skin beneath the chin, called a dewlap. When they are defending their terri- tory, or courting a female, they extend the pink flap like a little flag, and bob their head up and down. It looks like they're doing push-ups.

If a predator grabs one of these lizards by the tail, the tail breaks off. This allows the anole to escape. The tail will grow back, but a little shorter than the original.

Green Anole
Anolis carolinensis
(Southeastern US)

Gila Monster

Gila Monsters are the only venomous lizard in the United States. At 2 feet long, they are also the largest. They live in deserts and dry woodlands in the Southwest.

The lizards feed mostly on eggs they take from low-nesting birds, but they also eat a large variety of creatures. Their venom is used more as a defense than to subdue prey. If threatened, they bite. The grooved teeth create an open wound and as the lizard chews, venom in the saliva flows into that wound. In humans, it is rarely fatal, but very painful!

Gila Monster
Heloderma suspectum
(Southwestern US)

Gila Monsters are slow-moving lizards and would rather be left alone than chew on your finger. Their numbers are decreasing due to development, and they are protected in some states.

GLOSSARY

Abdomen: The rear body section on an arthropod. It contains the digestive system and reproductive organs.

Antenna: Jointed "feelers" located in pairs on the heads of insects.

Anticoagulant: A substance that keeps blood flowing.

Aquatic: Lives in water.

Arthropod: A segmented creature with jointed limbs that lacks an internal skeleton.

Burrow: A hole in the ground used as shelter by some animals.

Carcass: The dead body of an animal.

Castings: The waste product of worms.

Chitin: The main substance found in the outer layer of arthropods.

Crustacean: A variety of animals, including crabs, shrimp, and pillbugs, with a segmented body, hard outer shell, and paired, jointed limbs.

Dewlap: A fold of skin beneath the neck of certain animals.

Forcipules: The venom-injecting pincer-like front legs in centipedes.

Froglets: Young frogs.

Gland: An organ that secretes a fluid.

Hermaphrodite: Having both male and female reproductive organs.

Invertebrate: Lacking an internal skeleton.

Larva (Larvae, plural): Early, wormlike stage of an insect.

Nymph: Early, wingless, stage of an insect.

Pheromones: A chemical, or mix of chemicals, some animals use to communicate with one another.

Pincers: A pair of pointed structures on the head or tail used for grabbing.

Segment: In animals, it is a single section of a body that is joined by other sections.

Species: A group of individuals that have common traits.

Thorax: The middle section of an insect. It supports the legs and wings.

Tympanic Membrane: A thin skin-like layer that captures vibrations in the ear. It is also called an eardrum.

Venom: Poisonous fluid secreted or injected by some animals. An animal that produces venom is said to be venomous.

Vernal: Occurring in the spring.

INDEX

ABOUT THE AUTHOR

When John Himmelman was 8 years old, he started his first "Bug Club" in a friend's garage. They collected many of the creatures found in this book and created a bug zoo using various jars and containers. He's been playing with insects ever since.

Himmelman is an author and illustrator of many books for children. He graduated from the School of Visual Arts in Manhattan, New York. In his last year of college, he took a course in children's book writing and illustration, where he wrote *Talester the Lizard*. It became his first published book. He's also written books on amphibians and insects for "grown-up children." He is an amateur entomologist, herpetologist, and birder and travels North America giving talks on these and other topics. He is also a martial artist and co-runs a school in his town.

Living in the rural town of Killingworth, Connecticut, Himmelman finds many of his most exciting creatures in his own backyard. He often gets together with friends who also enjoy spending a day, or night, searching for wildlife. They call themselves the "Corps of Discovery," based upon the name of Lewis and Clark's expedition.

His wife, Betsy, is an art teacher, and they have two children. Jeffrey is an artist, and Lizzie is an actress. John's dog, a rat terrier named Jimmy, often joins him in the field.

Visit John Himmelman's main website at www.johnhimmelman.com. He also has a site on amphibians at www.ctamphibians.com and moths at www.connecticutmoths.com.

FALCON POCKET GUIDES
Nature in Your Pocket™

Birds of Arizona

A FALCON FIELD GUIDE

TODD TELANDER

Birds of Texas

A FALCON FIELD GUIDE

TODD TELANDER

Edible Wild Plants

A FALCON FIELD GUIDE

TODD TELANDER

FALCON POCKET GUIDES

Animal Tracks • Birds of Alaska • Birds of Arizona

Birds of California • Birds of Colorado • Birds of Florida

Birds of North Carolina • Birds of South Carolina

Birds of Texas • Birds of Virginia • Birds of West Virginia

Bison • Butterflies & Moths • Elk • Edible Wild Plants

Grizzly Bears • Mushrooms • Night Sky • Trees • Wolves

Available wherever books are sold!

falcon.com

To order, contact us
800.243.0495